20th Century Lives

SPORTING
HEROES

Jane Bingham

WAYLAND

First published in 2009 by Wayland

Copyright © Wayland 2009

This paperback edition published in 2012 by Wayland

Wayland
338 Euston Road
London NW1 3BH

Wayland
Hachette Children's Books
Level 17/207 Kent Street
Sydney, NSW 2000

Designer Jason Billin
Editor Nicola Edwards
Picture researcher: Louise Edgeworth

British Library Cataloguing in Publication Data
Bingham, Jane.
Sporting heroes. -- (20th century lives)
1. Sports--Biography--Juvenile literature. 2. Athletes--
Biography--Juvenile literature.
I. Title II. Series
796'.0922-dc22

ISBN 978-0-7502-6770-0

Printed in China

Wayland is a division of Hachette Children's Books, an Hachette UK Company.

Picture acknowledgements:
Cover: PA Photos/PA Archive; title page: Rex Features: CSU Archives/Everett Collection
Alamy: John Fryer p20, The Photolibrary Wales p21, Aflo Photo Agency/Alamy p27; Corbis:
Bettman p6, p7, p11, p15 & p26. George Tiedemann/GT Images p13, Schlegelmilch p18, Dimitri
Lundt/TempSport p22; Getty Images: Shaun Botterill/Allsport p2 & p17, Allsport/Hulton Archive
p8, Fox Photos p9, Frederick M Brown p16, David Cannon p24, Bob Thomas p28, Jerry
Wachter/NBAE via Getty Images p29; PA Photos: Panoramic p4 & p12, Gareth Copley/PA Archive
p5, PA Archive p14, Neal Simpson/Empics Sport p23, Presse Sports p25; Rex Features: CSU
Archives/Everett Collection p1 & p10, Sipa Press p19.

Contents

The Brazilian footballer Pelé celebrates after scoring his thousandth goal. This famous goal is sometimes known as O Milésimo and was scored in Brazil's Maracanã Stadium in 1969.

Pelé dedicated his thousandth goal to the poor children of Brazil. Many sports heroes have used their fame, skill and wealth to help others.

What makes a sporting hero?

When soccer legend Pelé scored his thousandth goal, people all over the world went wild. They knew that they were watching one of the most outstanding athletes of all time. Since he was a teenager, Pelé had astonished everyone who saw him play with his skill, speed and style.

Sporting heroes like Pelé make our lives more exciting. They provide an inspiring example to other athletes. They also demonstrate that it is possible to achieve some truly extraordinary feats.

What does it take?

All sporting heroes have incredible skills. But simply being skilful is not enough. In order to be the best, athletes need to train incredibly hard, devoting most of their time and energy to practising their sport.

In all sports people risk painful injuries. They can also face some serious disappointments and setbacks. Yet, despite these obstacles, sporting heroes do not give up. They keep trying to achieve the best they possibly can.

20th-century sport

The 16 men and women featured in this book are some of the greatest names in 20th-century sport. They represent a wide range of sports and nationalities. They also reflect the ways that sport has changed over the last hundred years.

In the early 20th century, many sports heroes were amateurs, and even professionals were not very well paid, but, by the 1980s, most sports had

become dominated by professionals. Leading sports men and women had become celebrities, who could expect to earn vast sums of money. At the same time, the number of women competitors grew very fast, and opportunities increased for disabled athletes.

Tanni Grey-Thompson is a leading wheelchair athlete from Wales. She has competed in five Paralympics, winning 16 medals, including 11 golds. The idea of holding a Paralympic Games for disabled athletes had its origins in 1948, and the first Olympic-style event took place in Rome in 1960.

A lasting legacy

The sporting heroes of the 20th century have left a great legacy for the future. Some of them have set records that have not yet been matched. Some have taken their sport in fresh directions and attracted new audiences. Most important of all, they have all provided an inspiring example to the athletes that have come after them.

"We all have dreams. But in order to make dreams come into reality it takes an awful lot of determination, dedication, self-discipline and effort." *Jesse Owens*

Babe Ruth

One of the greatest ever baseball players

"You just can't beat the person who never gives up."

Babe Ruth

A tough childhood

Babe Ruth came from a very poor family in the town of Baltimore, USA. His father, George Herman Ruth, Sr, ran a series of bars. His busy job left him with little time to spend with his young family. Babe's mother, Kate Schamberger-Ruth, was ill with tuberculosis (a serious lung disease). She died when Babe was a teenager. Of his seven brothers and sisters, only one sister, Marnie, survived to be an adult.

When Babe was seven years old, his father sent him to St Mary's Industrial School for boys, a very tough boarding school run by Catholic priests. He stayed there for the next 12 years, and only visited his family for special occasions.

A life-changing influence

Babe found it hard to cope with the strict environment of the school and was criticised for his bad behaviour. However, Brother Matthias, the school's Prefect of Discipline, was to have a very positive effect on Babe's behaviour. The priest became a father figure for Babe, making sure that he learnt to read and write, and coaching him in baseball. Babe developed a great talent for the game, both as a left-handed pitcher and as a powerful hitter. He played for the school team, in a variety of positions but most often as catcher.

Name George Herman Ruth, Jr

Nickname Babe Ruth. He was given his nickname when he started playing professional baseball aged 19.

Born 6 February, 1895 in Baltimore, Maryland, USA

Died 16 August 1948

Personal life He married twice and had two daughters.

High point In 1927, he became the first baseball player to hit 60 home runs in one season.

Low point In 1917, he punched an umpire and was suspended for 10 games.

Surprising fact When he was ill with stomach problems in 1925, it was such big news that journalists called it 'the bellyache that was heard all over the world'.

From Baltimore to Boston

At the age of 19, Babe's talent was spotted by a scout and he was chosen to play for the Baltimore Orioles. Less than six months later, he was sold to the Boston Red Sox. He played for the Red Sox for the next five years, and became famous for his fast pitching and his amazing swing. Babe could hit the ball harder and faster than anyone had done before.

Yankees' superstar

In 1919, Babe Ruth joined the New York Yankees. His career for the Yankees lasted 15 years and consisted of over 2,000 games. In this period, he achieved many baseball records. For example, in 1927, he became the first player to achieve 60 home runs (running all the way round the pitch in one go) within a single season. This record stayed unbroken for the next 34 years.

With Babe Ruth as the star atraction in the team, number of Yankees fans grew and grew. In 1923 the club built the famous Yankee Stadium, which became known as 'the house that Babe built'.

Later years

In 1935, the 40-year-old Babe transferred to the Boston Braves, but the following year he announced his retirement. By that time, his career total of 714 home runs was a world record, and was 336 more than the total of the next player.

After he retired, Babe became a radio star, often hosting a baseball quiz. He also had made several appearances in films, usually playing himself. He died from cancer at the age of 53.

Babe Ruth, playing for the Yankees, watches a ball that he has just hit sail towards the outfield wall. He was famous for his powerful swing.

Twentieth-century legacy

Babe Ruth turned baseball into a high-scoring power sport, and made it popular all over the world. He was one of the first international sports stars. People in many countries knew his name and a popular chocolate bar was named after him.

Donald Bradman

Cricket's greatest ever batsman

"I was never coached; I was never told how to hold a bat."

Donald Bradman

Early practice

Don Bradman spent his childhood in Bowral, a small country town in New South Wales, Australia. He was the youngest of five children, and spent a lot of his childhood playing alone.

As a young boy, Don invented a solo cricket game, using a a stump of wood to hit a golf ball against a curved brick wall, and then trying to hit the ball again when it bounced off the wall. This early practice helped him to develop excellent timing and incredibly fast reactions.

A brilliant start

At the age of 14 Don went to work in an estate agent's office, but he also played cricket for Bowral, and in 1926 he was selected for the state team of New South Wales. In his very first state match, aged 19, he achieved a century (100 runs).

Breaking records

In the following year, he began playing in Test matches for Australia. Before he was 22 he had set many batting records, some of which are still unbeaten today. During this time Don gained a reputation for a very exciting batting style, sometimes using strokes that reminded the spectators of golf or tennis.

Name Sir Donald George Bradman

Nickname The Don

Born 27 August 1908 in Cootamundra, New South Wales, Australia

Died 25 February 2001

Personal life He married in 1932 and had two sons and a daughter.

High point In a match in1930, he scored an astonishing 974 runs, a record that is still unbeaten.

Low point In his last Test match, in 1948, he was bowled out on the second ball.

Surprising fact He learnt to play cricket on concrete wickets covered with matting, and did not bat and run on grass until he was 18.

Great achievements

Altogether, Don played for Australia for 20 years, but in 1934 he missed a year of play when he became very ill with appendicitis. However, he soon returned to top form. In the third Test match against England in 1937, he made 270 runs. This score has been rated as the greatest innings of all time.

Spectators at the Headingly ground in Leeds applaud Donald Bradman as he comes out to bat for Australia during a Test match in 1938.

During World War Two (1939-1945), international cricket stopped, but, after the war, Don played for Australia for three more years, before retiring in 1948 at the age of 40. At the end of his career, he had achieved an average in Test cricket matches of 99.94 runs, over 40 runs more than anyone has ever managed since.

Private life

Away from the cricket pitch, Don lived a quiet life in a small house in Adelaide. He and his wife Jessie were married for 65 years. The family suffered several tragedies. Don and Jessie's first son died as a baby, their second son caught polio and was paralysed for a year, and their daughter was born with cerebral palsy (a condition that causes severe paralysis).

In 1949 Don was knighted by the Queen. He was the first cricketer to be honoured in this way for his services to the sport.

Twentieth-century legacy

Donald Bradman is Australia's greatest sporting hero. In 2001 the Australian prime minister called him the 'greatest living Australian'. With his exciting, attacking style, Bradman drew record crowds to watch cricket matches. He has inspired generations of cricketers. The former captain of the Australian cricket team, Steve Waugh, has described Bradman as 'a once-in a lifetime player'.

Jesse Owens

One of the first great African-American athletes

"We all have dreams. But in order to make dreams come into reality it takes an awful lot of determination, dedication, self-discipline and effort."

Jesse Owens

A young athlete

Jesse Owens grew up in the Oakville community of black Americans, close to Cleveland, Alabama. His family was poor and Jesse had to take a range of jobs, such as delivering groceries and repairing shoes. At school, he was encouraged to join the running team. He practised early in the morning, so he could work after school. He went on to become a champion athlete in track and field events, such as the sprint and the long jump.

Record beater

When he was 22, Jesse won a place at Ohio State University. As a member of the university athletics team, he competed in national competitions, winning many medals. In one competition in Ann Arbor, Michigan in 1935, Jesse managed a remarkable set of achievements. He equalled the world record for the 100-yard (91-metre) sprint, and set world records in the long jump, the 220-yard (201.2-m) sprint, and the low hurdles events.

Name James Cleveland Owens

Nickname Jesse. He was called Jesse at school, when he said his name was 'J.C.'.

Born 12 September 1913 in Oakville, Alabama, USA

Died 31 March 1980

Personal life Jesse married in 1935 and he had three daughters.

High point In 1936, he became the first American to win four Olympic gold medals in track and field events.

Low point After Jesse's Olympic victories, Adolf Hitler, the Chancellor of Germany, did not shake his hand, and President F D Roosevelt failed to congratulate him. Jesse was very upset about this obvious racism.

Surprising fact As an Olympic hero, Jesse was given a party in a New York hotel, but he was not allowed to ride in the same elevator as his white guests.

Jesse Owens astonished the crowds at the Berlin Olympics with his skill, speed and style. He is shown here performing the long jump.

An Olympic hero

The 1936 Olympic Games were run by Adolf Hitler's Nazi Party. Hitler had planned to use the Olympics to show that German athletes were the best, but during the Games it was Jesse Owens who really stunned the crowds. He won the 100-metre sprint, the long jump, and the 200-metre sprint. He was also part of the American team that won the 100-metre relay race. Hitler was furious, and said that black athletes should be disqualified in future. However, many German people saw Jesse as a hero.

After the Olympics

Jesse did not compete in any more major events. In that period it was very hard for black people to be accepted in white society. For the next 20 years, he struggled to earn a living. Then, in the 1960s, Jesse began a career as speaker. He travelled the world encouraging people to achieve their best.

Twentieth-century legacy

At the Berlin Olympics, Jesse showed the world what a black athlete could achieve. He has become a hero for black competitors in all sports. Following his death in 1980, the Jesse Owens Foundation was set up in Ohio to encourage young people to develop their full potential.

Name Edison Arantes do Nascimento

Nickname Pelé. He was given this nickname by friends at school.

Born 23 October 1940 in Três Corações, Brazil

Personal life He has been married twice and has seven children.

High point On 19 November 1969, Pelé scored his thousandth goal in all competitions. He dedicated it to the poor children of Brazil.

Low point In the 1962 World Cup, Pelé was injured in the second round so he could not play in the final match.

Surprising fact In Nigeria in 1968, a two-day truce was declared in the war with Biafra so that both sides could watch Pelé play.

Pelé

The greatest footballer of all time

"Enthusiasm is everything. It must be taut and vibrating like a guitar string."

Pelé

A poor childhood

Pelé's family lived in the town of Bauru, Brazil. His father was a footballer who had to retire early, and he coached his son. The family was very poor, and Pelé earned extra money as a shoeshine boy. When he was young, his family could not afford a proper football for Pelé to practise with, so he used a grapefruit or a sock stuffed with newspaper.

By the time he reached his teens, Pelé had developed amazing skills at tackling and passing, taking headers and scoring goals. Aged 15, he was picked for the Santos FC junior team and after just one season he joined the senior team.

A brilliant career

In his first season playing for Santos, the 16-year-old Pelé was the top scorer in the Brazilian league. In the following year, at the age of 17, he became the youngest player ever to play in a World Cup Final, scoring two goals for Brazil. After the World Cup, European clubs offered massive fees to sign the young player, but the government of Brazil declared Pelé an 'official national treasure' to prevent him being signed up by another country.

Pelé played for Santos until 1974 and was Brazil's star player in a team that contained many talented members. He played as an inside forward and a striker and in the vital playmaker position, controlling his team's attacking play. In his 22-year career, Pelé scored 1,281 goals and was the only footballer to play in three World Cup winning teams. He became an international footballing

For three years in the 1970s the American public had the chance to see Pelé in action, playing for the New York Cosmos. He is shown here in a match against the Washington Diplomats.

legend, famous for his elegant playing style, his astonishing speed, and his remarkable ball control.

Later life

In 1975 Pelé signed up with the New York Cosmos, and played three seasons for them, helping to raise American interest in football. Since his retirement from football in 1977, he has run businesses, performed in films, and campaigned on a range of issues, including ecology and the environment.

Twentieth-century legacy

Pelé has inspired generations of young footballers everywhere, but especially in the less-developed countries of the world. He has shown the world what a beautiful game football can be when it is played with such incredible skill.

Muhammad Ali

Three-times Heavyweight Boxing World Champion

"Float like a butterfly, sting like a bee."

Muhammad Ali

Starting young

Until he was 22, Muhammad Ali was called Cassius Clay. He grew up in Louisville, USA, where his father was a signpainter and his mother worked as a cleaner. At the age of 12, he started learning to box and was soon winning amateur titles.

In 1960, at the age of 18, Ali won the Olympic Light Heavyweight gold medal. Following this triumph, he returned to Louisville to begin his professional career. At the end of his time as an amateur, he had won a hundred fights and lost only five.

Religion and war

Between 1960 and 1963, Ali fought 19 matches and won them all. He gained a reputation as a very stylish fighter, who was incredibly light on his feet and speedy with his punches. At the same time he became famous for his self-confidence, bragging before matches and taunting his opponents.

In 1964 Ali had his first professional title fight, beating Sonny Liston to become the World Heavyweight Boxing Champion. Later that year, he announced his conversion to Islam and changed his name to Muhammad Ali. In 1967, he refused to

Name Muhammad Ali

Original name Cassius Marcellus Clay Junior. Ali changed his name in 1964 when he converted to the Muslim religion.

Born 17 January 1942 in Louisville, Kentucky, USA

Personal life He has been married four times and has seven daughters and two sons.

High point In 1974, Ali won a surprise victory against George Foreman, in a thrilling fight in Zaire, known as 'the rumble in the jungle'.

Low point In 1975, he fought an exhibition match against Antonio Inoki, who concentrated his attack on Ali's legs. The result was a draw, but Ali's legs were permanently weakened.

Surprising fact The singer Frank Sinatra was so desperate to see the Ali-Frazier fight in 1971 that he agreed to photograph the fight for *Match* magazine.

In 1965, Muhammad Ali fought Sonny Liston to defend his title as World Heavyweight Champion. Ali knocked Liston out after one minute in the first round. In this photograph, Liston is shown struggling to recover, but soon after this the referee decided that Ali had won the fight.

join the US army and fight in the Vietnam War. As a result of this he was put on trial and banned from professional boxing.

Wins and losses

In 1970, Ali was allowed to fight again. A year later, he was defeated by Joe Frazier in a fight promoted as 'the fight of the century'. However, in 1974 he regained his World Heavyweight title when he beat George Foreman. Ali lost his title in February 1978, when he was beaten by Leon Spinks, but, seven months later, he won the title back from Spinks.

Later life

In 1979, Ali retired from professional boxing. Since then he has campaigned for many causes, especially world peace, understanding and respect. In 1984, he was diagnosed with Parkinson's Disease (a condition that makes people shake uncontrollably) but he has continued with his campaigning work.

Twentieth-century legacy

Through his self-promotion and his skill in the ring, Ali turned boxing into a very popular spectator sport. He is the world's most famous African-American sports personality and he has helped to inspire many black athletes.

Steffi Graf

The greatest female tennis player of the 20th century

"As long as I can focus on enjoying what I'm doing, having fun, I know I'll play well."

Steffi Graf

Early promise

Steffi Graf grew up in the town of Mannheim, Germany. She was taught to play tennis by her father, who showed her how to swing a racket when she was only three. By the time she was four she was practising on a court and she played in her first tournament when she was five. She soon began winning junior championships, and in 1982, aged 13, she played in her first adult professional tennis tournament.

Rising through the ranks

During her early years as a young professional player, Steffi's father made sure that she did not 'burn out' by playing too many matches. He also insisted that she should concentrate on practising her tennis rather than attending social events. In her first year in professional tennis, Steffi was ranked as world number 124. Within three years she had risen to world number 6, at the age of 16.

Grand Slams

In 1986, Steffi won her first World Tennis Association tournament, beating Chris Evert. The following year, she won several tournaments and in 1988 she

Name Stefanie Maria Graf

Nickname Steffi

Born 14 June 1969 in Mannheim, Germany

Personal life She is married to the American tennis champion, André Agassi, and has a son and a daughter.

High point In 1988, Steffi won an Olympic gold medal for singles tennis, just one week after achieving the 'Calendar Year Grand Slam' (see main text). Journalists called it the 'Golden Slam'.

Low point In 1995, she was accused of not paying enough tax. Her father, who had managed her money, went to jail for two years and Steffi had to pay a large fine.

Surprising fact Steffi's husband, André Agassi, claims he had been secretly pining for her since 1990. They got married in 2001.

achieved a 'Calendar Year Grand Slam', winning all four 'Grand Slam' titles (the Australian Open, the French Open, Wimbledon and the US Open).

She proved herself to be equally skilful on all playing surfaces, and she became famous for her hard-hitting style. Over the next two years, she continued to win many Grand Slam titles, but 1991-1992 was a difficult period as she suffered illness and injuries.

Injuries and achievements

From 1993 to 1996, Steffi returned to winning form, but she also suffered from serious back problems, sometimes having to wear a brace between matches. An injured knee meant that she could not take part in the Summer Olympics of 1996 and she missed many matches over the next two years due to injury.

Retirement and beyond

In 1999, Steffi announced her retirement from international tennis, even though she was still ranked number three in the world. This made her the highest-ranked player to announce retirement from the sport since computerized records began. During her career, she had won an astonishing total of 22 Grand Slam singles titles.

Steffi now supports several charities, including the Worldwide Fund for Nature, for which she is an international ambassador. She has founded a youth tennis centre in Germany and a charity called Children for Tomorrow which supports children whose lives have been damaged by war.

Steffi Graf is famous for her powerful backhand strokes. She is shown here in action in the semi-finals of the 1996 US Open Tennis Championships. Steffi went on to win the competition.

Twentieth-century legacy

Steffi Graf demonstrated that a female tennis player could show great stamina, speed and skill on all playing surfaces. She also proved that it was possible for a woman player to have a very strong service. Her serve could reach speeds of 180 kpm (110 mph).

Ayrton Senna

Formula One champion and Brazilian national hero

"Each driver has his limit. My limit is a little bit further than others'."

Ayrton Senna

Starting young

Ayrton Senna was the son of a wealthy Brazilian landowner. As a boy he was very keen on the sport of motor kart racing and, at the age of 17, he won the South American Kart Championship. By the time he reached his twenties, Ayrton had become more interested in motor racing. In 1981, he moved to England to take up a career as a racing driver.

Formula One

In Britain, Ayrton quickly moved up the ranks of motor racing, winning the Formula Three championship in 1983. In the following year, he began Formula One racing, as a member of the Toleman team. In 1985, he moved to the Lotus-Renault team and over the next three seasons, he won a total of six Grand Prix races.

In 1988, Ayrton joined the McLaren-Honda team, where he developed a rivalry with his team-mate, Alain Prost. In the same year, he and Prost won 15 out of the 16 Grand Prix races of the season, and Ayrton won his first Formula One World Championship title (awarded to the driver with the highest number of points in the season). He

---

Name Ayrton Senna da Silva

Born 21 March 1960 in Sao Paolo, Brazil

Died 1 May 1994

Personal life Ayrton was a devout Christian who secretly donated large amounts of his winnings to poor Brazilian children.

High point In 1991, at Suzuka, in Japan, Ayrton realized he would win the World Championship even if he came second, so he slowed down to allow Gerhard Berger, his McLaren team-mate, to win.

Low point In 1989, the rivalry between Ayrton and Alain Prost led to a collision on the track at Suzuka. Ayrton went on to win the race, but he was disqualified and given a heavy fine.

Surprising fact Ayrton began racing when he took over a gift rejected by his older sister – a go-cart with a lawn-mower engine.

won the Championship again in 1990 and 1991. In 1992, the performance of the McLaren-Honda team began to decline, and in 1994, Ayrton signed up with the Williams-Renault team.

This photo shows Ayrton Senna racing for the Honda-McLaren team in 1991, three years before his fatal accident at the age of 34.

Danger at San Marino

Ayrton's third race with his new team was the San Marino Grand Prix, held at Imola in Italy. On the day before the race, Roland Ratzenberger, an Austrian driver, had been killed while he was practising on the track. Ayrton was very upset by Ratzenberger's death and he held a meeting with his fellow drivers. In the meeting, Ayrton volunteered to lead a group to increase safety in Formula One racing.

A fatal accident

Ayrton took the lead in the race, but on the seventh lap his car span out of control and crashed into a concrete barrier. He was airlifted to hospital where he was declared dead. In Brazil, the government announced three days of national mourning and more than a million people attended his burial.

Twentieth-century legacy

Ayrton's death on the track led to many improvements in motor racing safety. Since 1994, most tracks have been redesigned to make them safer, and better crash barriers have been installed. Ayrton is also remembered in the Insituto Ayrton Senna. After he died, it was discovered that he had donated millions of dollars to help poor children in Brazil, and the Instituto continues this work.

Tanni Grey-Thompson

Paralympian wheelchair athlete

"I like pushing myself to the limit."
Tanni Grey-Thompson

Early life

Tanni Grey-Thompson comes from Cardiff, in Wales. She was born with spina bifida, a medical condition in which the spine is not properly formed. This meant she was paralysed from the waist down. As a small girl she had to wear callipers to support her legs, and when she was seven she began to use a wheelchair. However, her disability did not stop her from trying out sports. While at school she especially enjoyed swimming, archery and horse-riding.

Wheelchair racer

At the age of 13, Tanni started wheelchair racing, and two years later she won the 100-metre race at the Junior National Wheelchair Games. When she was 18, she was selected for the British Wheelchair Racing Squad. In 1988, at the age of 19, Tanni won a bronze medal at the Seoul Paralympics. Over the next few years, she had some major back surgery but was also able to study for a degree in politics at Loughborough University and keep up her training as a wheelchair racer.

Great achievements

At the Barcelona Paralympics, in 1992, Tanni won four gold medals in the 100-, 200-, 400- and 800-metre races. Later the same year, she won her first

Name Dame Carys Davina Grey-Thompson

Nickname Tanni. When her older sister first saw baby Carys she called her "Tiny", which she pronounced as "Tanni".

Born 26 July 1969 in Cardiff, Wales

Personal life In 1999 Tanni married Ian Thompson, who is also a wheelchair athlete. They have one daughter.

High point Winning four gold medals at the Sydney Paralympics in 2000.

Low point In 1989, the year after her first Paralympics, Tanni had to miss a year of sport while she had surgery on her spine.

Surprising fact Tanni's racing chair is made to fit her exactly. She can only fit into it when she is wearing her lycra racing suit.

Tanni Grey-Thompson competes in the 800-metre race during the Welsh Senior Championship and Cardiff Centenary Games. The Games were held in 2005 at the Leckwith Stadium in Tanni's home city of Cardiff.

London Wheelchair Marathon. Since then, she has won the Marathon five more times, and has competed in five Paralympics, winning 16 medals, including 11 golds.

In 2005 Tanni was made a Dame Commander of the Order of the British Empire in recognition of her outstanding services to sport. Two years later, she retired from athletics at the age of 35, but she still plays a very active part in promoting sports in Britain.

Anti-drug campaigner

Tanni is a strong supporter of strict drug tests for athletes. In 2008 she was asked to investigate government policies on drugs in sport. Her report recommended that the UK government should make more efforts to prevent the use of performance-enhancing drugs by athletes.

Twentieth-century legacy

In her career, Tanni showed what could be achieved through determination and self-belief. She is an inspiration to all athletes, and especially to those with disabilities. She is also helping to make sport free from drugs.

Jonah Lomu

First global superstar of rugby union

"I think everyone has a pure, natural talent. The responsibility on the individual is to grow with it and enhance it."

Jonah Lomu

Early career

Jonah Lomu's family orginally came from the island of Tonga, and he grew up in a poor district of Auckland, New Zealand. At school, Jonah excelled in sport and, when he was 14, he was invited to join a team of promising teenagers playing rugby union.

International star

In 1994, at the age of 19, Jonah played his first international match for the New Zealand All Blacks. In the following year, he took part in the Rugby World Cup, scoring an amazing seven tries in five matches.

On the pitch, Jonah stood out from all the other players because of his size and strength – he is 1.96 metres (6ft 5inches) tall and weighs 120 kg. He could also run extremely fast and had the ability to bulldoze his way through an opposing team's defence.

In 1996, Jonah was a key member of the team that became the first champions of the newly-created

Name Jonah Tali Lomu

Born 12 May 1975 in Auckland, New Zealand

Personal life Jonah has been married and divorced twice. He lives with his third partner who gave birth to Jonah's first child in 2009.

High point In 1995, he scored four tries in the World Cup semi-final against England.

Low point In 2003, Jonah's doctor told him he would end up in a wheelchair if he did not have a kidney transplant soon.

Surprising fact Each of Jonah's thighs has a circumference of 33 inches – the size of an average man's waist.

Tri Nations Series. This competition was held between the three nations of New Zealand, Australia and South Africa. Jonah scored in the match against Australia which New Zealand won by 32 points to 25.

Health problems

Ever since he was a boy, Jonah had fought against extreme tiredness, relying on his incredible will power to carry him through rugby matches. Then, at the end of 1996, the cause of his problems was discovered. He was diagnosed with a rare kidney disease and given emergency treatment in hospital.

Jonah missed the 1997 Series but he was back playing international rugby later that year. In 1998 he won a gold medal representing New Zealand in the sevens rugby event of the Commonwealth Games, held at Kuala Lumpur in Malaysia.

Over the next few years, Jonah continued to play as much as he could, including his star performance in the World Cup in 1995 (see panel on page 22). However, his kidney disease grew gradually worse and by 2003 he needed kidney dialysis treatment for eight hours a day several times a week.

Recovery, injury and retirement

In 2004, Jonah was given a kidney transplant, and by 2005 he was playing international rugby again. Since then, he has suffered several injuries, and, in 2007, he announced his retirement.

Jonah Lomu is a powerfully built athlete who is famous for his speed on the pitch, but he has had to battle with serious kidney disease. At one stage he described himself as being "so sick I couldn't even run past a little baby".

Twentieth-century legacy

Jonah's massive size and powerful attacking style added an element of drama to rugby union, bringing many new fans to the sport. Jonah has also been an inspiring example to others through his courageous struggle against ill health.

Jack Nicklaus

The greatest professional golfer of all time

A young golfer

Jack Nicklaus was the son of a pharmacist and grew up in the suburb of Upper Arlington, close to Columbus, USA. He started playing golf when he was ten years old. In his early teens he had a mild case of polio (a disease that can leave people partly paralysed) and began to practise golf very seriously to help himself recover.

When Jack was 16 years old he won the Ohio State Open Golf Championship, and at the age of 20 he came second in the US Open.

Jack the champion

In 1962, Jack turned professional, and later that year he won the US Open, starting a long career of championship wins. Between the years 1962 and 1986 he won an amazing total of 18 major championships in 25 seasons. Throughout his long career, he was famous for his long, straight drives.

Later career

In 1986, at the age of 46, Jack won his sixth Masters Cup victory, becoming the oldest person to win the cup, a record that still stands. Jack finally retired from professional golf in 2005, at the age of 65. He now spends much of his time designing golf courses.

Name Jack William Nicklaus

Nickname The Golden Bear

Born 21 January 1940 in Columbus, Ohio, USA

Personal life He is married and has five children.

High point In 1978, he achieved a 'career Grand Slam', becoming the only player to have won all four major golf championships three times.

Low point In 1968 and 1969 Jack did not win an Open, but, by 1970, he was playing even better than before.

Eddy Merckx

The most successful cyclist of the 20th century

Early career

Eddy Merckx was the son of a grocer in Brussels, Belgium. At the age of eight, he was given a second-hand racing bike and, by the time he was 16, he was winning cycle club races. In 1964 he became the world amateur cycling champion and the following year he turned professional.

Riding to victory

In 1966, the 20-year-old Eddy won the Milan-San Remo race. This was followed by a series of victories, but his major breakthrough came in 1969 when he won the *Tour de France* (the most important road cycling race in the world). In this race, he won the yellow jersey for overall leader, the green jersey for best sprinter and the red polka-dotted jersey for best climber in the mountains. No other rider has achieved this triple in the *Tour de France*.

Record-breaker

Between 1968 and 1974, Eddy won a record eleven Grand Tours (the three biggest road races in the cycling word, held in France, Italy and Spain). In 1972, he broke the record for the longest distance cycled in one hour. His distance of 49.431km (30.715 miles) remained unbeaten for 12 years. Eddy retired in 1978, at the age of 32.

Name Baron Edouard Louis Joseph Merckx

Born 17 June1945 in Meensel-Kiezegem, Belgium

Personal life He is married and has a son and a daughter.

High point In 1974, Eddy won the *Giro d'Italia*, the *Tour de France* and the World Championship Road Race to achieve the 'Triple Crown' in cycling.

Low point In 1969, he was involved in an accident when he and his pacer (a cyclist who helps another to keep up a certain speed for part of a race) were forced to fall. The pacer was killed instantly and Eddy suffered serious injuries.

Mark Spitz

Record-breaking Olympic swimmer

Young talent

When Mark Spitz was two years old, his family moved to Hawaii and he went swimming every day. In 1956, the family returned to California and at the age of nine Mark started training seriously. While he was at high school, he held national high school records in every stroke and at every distance, but his greatest strengths were freestyle (front crawl) and butterfly.

Winning at swimming

In 1966, aged 16, Mark won the 100-metre butterfly race in the American national championships. This was the first of a total of 24 national titles that he would win. Between 1968 and 1972, he won five Pan American gold medals and set 33 world records. He was named World Swimmer of the Year in 1969, 1971 and 1972.

Olympic champion

In 1968, Mark won two gold medals for freestyle at the Mexico Summer Olympics. He was disappointed with this achievement as he was sure he could do better. His great triumph came in 1972 at the Munich Olympics. There, he won four individual events in freestyle and butterfly, and three relay races. His record of seven Olympic golds in one competition was unbeaten until Michael Phelps won eight golds in 2008. After the Olympics, Mark retired from competition and had a brief career as a media celebrity.

Name Mark Andrew Spitz

Nickname Mark the Shark

Born 10 February 1950 in Modesto, California, USA

Personal life He is married and has two sons.

High point In 1972 Mark won seven gold medals in the Munich Olympic Games.

Low point In the 1968 Summer Olympics, Mark predicted he would win six gold medals, but only won two.

Yasuhiro Yamashita

The greatest judo champion of the 20th century

Early promise

Yasuhiro Yamashita grew up in the town of Yamato, Japan. He began studying judo while he was at primary school and by the time he moved to senior school he had already gained his black belt (a sign of the most senior level of skill). At the age of 19, he became the youngest competitor in history to win the All-Japan Judo Championship title.

Many victories

In 1979, Yasuhiro won a gold medal at the World Judo Championships. Between the years 1977 and 1985, he won 203 victories and was unbeaten in any competition. His achievements during this time included four World Championship titles.

In his contests, Yasuhiro made excellent use of his heavy build and his left-handed stance and he was equally skilled in standing and ground moves. Many of his victories were due to his hold or choke moves, executed on an opponent lying on the ground.

An honoured teacher

In 1984, Yasuhiro received the Japanese National Prize of Honour and in the following year he retired from competitive judo. Since then, he has worked as head coach for the Japanese national judo team.

Yasuhiro Yamashita is seen here at the 2008 Olympics in Beijing. He was involved in helping the Chinese men's judo team to prepare for the competition.

Name Yasuhiro Yamashita

Born 1 June 1957 in Kumamato Prefecture, Kyushu, Japan

Personal life Yasuhiro is married and has two sons and a daughter.

High point In April 1985, he won the All-Japan Championships for the ninth time in a row.

Low point In the finals of the 1980 All-Japan Championships, Yasuhiro's leg was broken by his opponent and the match was declared a draw.

27

Jayne Torvill & Christopher Dean

World-famous ice-dancing duo

Starting out

Jayne Torvill and Christopher Dean both grew up in Nottinghamshire, England. Jayne took up skating at the age of eight and Christopher began when he was ten. As teenagers they both won junior championships with other partners, but their careers took off in 1975, when they started dancing together. Soon they were winning national competitions as a duo.

Taking skating seriously

After they left school, Christopher and Jayne started working at full-time jobs, and it was hard for them to find time to practise. In the 1980 Winter Olympics, they came fifth in the ice-dancing event and decided it was time to give up their jobs and concentrate full-time on their skating.

Olympic triumph

In the 1984 Winter Olympics, held in Sarajevo in the former Yugoslavia, Torvill and Dean won the gold medal for their dance to the music of Ravel's *Bolero*. Their performance was given the highest set of marks ever awarded to an ice-dance routine.

Later that year, they turned professional and could no longer compete in the Olympics. However, the rules were relaxed in 1994, when they won an Olympic bronze medal. The pair also performed in ice-dancing shows before retiring in 1998.

Name Jayne Torvill
Born 7 October 1957 in Nottingham, England
Personal life She is married with a son and a daughter.

Name Christopher Colin Dean
Born 27 July 1958 in Nottingham, England
Personal life He has been married twice and has two sons.

Michael Jordan

The greatest basketball player of all time

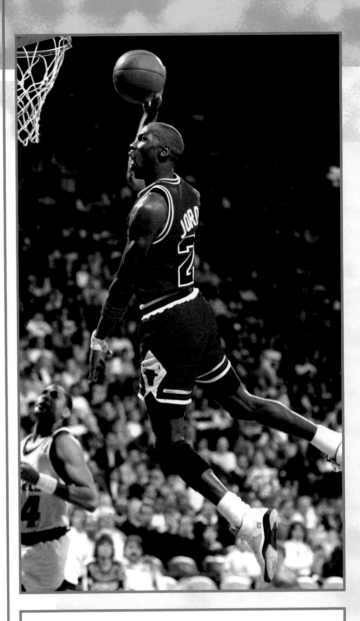

A young player

Michael Jordan grew up in North Carolina, USA. At school he was outstanding at baseball, football and basketball, but he finally decided to concentrate on basketball. During his last two seasons at high school, Jordan averaged 20 points per game and was selected for the McDonald's All-American Team. At the age of 18, he won a basketball scholarship to the University of North Carolina.

Star of the Bulls

In 1984 Michael joined the Chicago Bulls, soon becoming their star player both in goal scoring and defence. In 1991 he won his first NBA championship with the Bulls, and he later helped his team to win the championship five more times.

Michael stood out from the rest of the team because of his high jumps, and his amazing ability to score goals. He is especially famous for his slam dunks into the net.

Later career

In 1993, Michael retired from basketball to pursue a career in baseball, but returned in 1995 to play for the Bulls. He retired again in 1999, returning in 2001 to play two seasons for the Washington Wizards. After retiring from basketball for the third time, in 2003, Michael has had a successful business career.

Name Michael Jeffrey Jordan

Nickname Air Jordan

Born 17 February 1963 in Brooklyn, New York, USA

Personal life He is divorced and has two sons.

High point In 1990, Michael scored an all-time high of 69 points in a game against the Cleveland Cavaliers.

Low point In 1993, Michael was devastated when his father was murdered. Later that year, Michael announced his (first) retirement from basketball.

Timeline

1914 World War One begins.

1918 World War One ends.

1927 Babe Ruth becomes the first baseball player to hit 60 home runs in one season.

1930 Donald Bradman scores 974 runs in a single cricket match.

1936 Jesse Owens wins four gold medals for athletics at the Berlin Olympic Games run by Adolf Hitler's Nazi Party.

1939 World War Two begins.

1945 World War Two ends.

1964 Muhammad Ali becomes World Heavyweight Boxing Champion.

1969 Pelé scores the thousandth goal in his soccer career.

1972 Mark Spitz wins seven gold medals for swimming at the Munich Olympics.

1974 Eddy Merckx achieves the 'Tripe Crown' in cycling, winning all three major cycle races.

1978 Jack Nicklaus becomes the only player to have won all four major golf championships three times.

1984 Jayne Torvill and Christopher Dean win a gold medal for ice-dancing at the Sarajevo Winter Olympics.

1985 Yasushiro Yamashita wins the All-Japan Judo Championships for the ninth time in a row.

1988 Steffi Graf wins all four tennis Grand Slam titles.

1990 Michael Jordan scores an all-time high of 69 points in a basketball game for the Chicago Bulls.

1991 Ayrton Senna wins his third Formula One World Championship title.

1994 Ayrton Senna dies in a crash during the San Marino Grand Prix in Italy.

1995 Jonah Lomu scores four tries in a Rugby World Cup semi-finals match.

2000 Tanni Grey-Thompson wins four gold medals at the Sydney Paralympics.

Glossary

amateur Someone who takes part in a sport for pleasure, and is not paid for playing that sport.

backhand A stroke in tennis that is played with the back of the hand facing outwards and the arm across the body.

callipers Metal rods strapped onto someone's legs to strengthen them.

celebrities People who are very well-known.

defence Protection from attacks. In a team sport such as football, the defence tries to prevent the opposite team from scoring goals.

diagnose To work out what disease somebody has.

drive A drive in golf is a shot that is long, hard hit.

home run In baseball, a player achieves a home run when he or she runs all the way round the pitch in one go.

hurdles Small fences that athletes jump over in a running event.

installed Put in place, ready to be used.

kidney dialysis A medical treatment given to patients with serious kidney problems. The dialysis machine performs the functions of the kidneys and removes waste from the patient's body.

legacy Something that is left by someone to the people who come after him or her.

Nazi Party The party led by Adolf Hitler in Germany in the years leading up to World War Two.

outfield wall The wall at the edge of a baseball pitch.

pacer Someone who helps to keep up the pace of a cyclist in a race.

Paralympics An athletic competition for disabled athletes held in the same year as the Olympics.

paralysed Lacking in movement, feeling and power.

pitcher Some who throws (or bowls) a baseball to the batter.

polio An infectious disease that affects the brain and spine and which can make a person paralysed.

professional Someone who is paid for doing something, such as a sport, that many others do as amateurs.

racism Unfair treatment of others who belong to a different race.

relay race A team race in which members of the team take it in turns to run or swim.

run A point scored in cricket, made by a pair of batsmen running a short distance.

slam dunk A goal in basketball, scored by the player jumping into the air and pushing the ball downwards through the basket.

sprint A short, very fast race.

stroke A way of hitting the ball in tennis, or a method of moving in swimming.

swing A way of hitting a ball hard that involves swinging the bat through the air.

taunting Teasing.

Test matches Test matches in cricket are matches played between national teams.

track and field Athletic sports that involve running, jumping or throwing.

Vietnam War A war fought between the South Vietnamese government, supported by US troops, and the communist government of North Vietnam.

Index

Numbers in **bold** refer to pictures.